The 10 Most Popular
Un-American
Attitudes

The 10 Most Popular Un-American Attitudes

David Coleman

iUniverse, Inc.
New York Lincoln Shanghai

The 10 Most Popular Un-American Attitudes

iUniverse books may be ordered through booksellers or by contacting:

iUniverse
2021 Pine Lake Road, Suite 100
Lincoln, NE 68512
www.iuniverse.com
1-800-Authors (1-800-288-4677)

ISBN-13: 978-0-595-38704-5 (pbk)
ISBN-13: 978-0-595-83086-2 (ebk)
ISBN-10: 0-595-38704-7 (pbk)
ISBN-10: 0-595-83086-2 (ebk)

Printed in the United States of America

Contents

FOREWORD

I believe there are millions of Americans who agree with the arguments put forth in this book, but most of them don't feel qualified to speak out loudly. Well, I don't either, but that hasn't stopped me. The stakes are far too high to let this pass without trying to make a difference.

We need to re-examine our attitudes from a distance to see how far we have strayed from the principles on which this country was founded. There are so many conflicting ideas out there and so much information to digest, that I feel we often forget which path we should be following. It is easy to become confused in one's thinking.

Any of us can get caught up in a mass movement that slowly becomes accepted as normal. New trends do not always signify progress, and my book attempts to list the most common trends that are not good for America. I draw attention to a lot of today's attitudes that I believe many people accept without realizing how Un-American they really are. My objective is to reach those people who embrace these attitudes but perhaps have not realized that they are harmful to us all. By exposing these in simple language, it is my hope that more people will appreciate the need to adjust their attitudes.

America did not rise to the top of the heap with these attitudes, and we will not stay at the top very much longer with them. I fear that if we do not reverse these trends we will steadily lose ground in a very competitive world. We will slowly undermine the system that has worked so well for us in the past, and spiral into a country of mediocrity. In my frequent travels to third-world countries I perceive more and more examples where they are raising their standards while we are lowering ours. One could almost be excused for thinking we are aimlessly shooting at our own feet.

This is not a partisan book, and I make no distinction between Democrats and Republicans. Most of us hold opinions that span a wider spectrum than partisan politics would indicate. For those who disagree with me philosophically, I hold no real hope that this book will change your minds. For those who agree with me and who already are trying to change popular opinion, I can offer no specific encouragement. Just, please keep trying. I am fully aware that people don't change long-held attitudes overnight.

I wanted to keep this book simple and to the point, since there are countless books available which deal with each of these topics in far more detail and are written by people with more knowledge. The only problem is that most people don't read them. I expect my book will draw criticism from scholars of economics, politics, law, government and social engineering, but I didn't write it for them. This book is written by an ordinary man for other ordinary men and women. Most of us are ordinary people—decent, honest, compassionate, proud, and generally trying to do our best. We just want the truth. We frequently make mistakes, but we accept the consequences and get on with the show.

Some readers may be surprised to note that I have not used any references, and have not quoted any statistics. This is deliberate because I wanted the book to be straight from the heart and not a scholarly textbook or a replay of what has already been said so many times before.

I am a naturalized citizen and came here believing the American model was the only truly moral social model. I deplore the undermining of this model, some of it by design but mostly by apathy, complacency and misdirected attitudes. I make no apologies for raising controversial topics and hope to spark interest, debate and action. If anyone can change the prevailing attitudes it will be ordinary Americans. If we wait for someone else to do so, especially the government or the media, it will never happen.

The reader will inevitably find some overlap and duplication between the chapters—partly because many of these attitudes are inter-related and partly because many points need emphasizing at every opportunity.

Finally, one small disclaimer: for the sake of brevity, I use the term "America" synonymously with "United States of America". In no way is this meant as a put-down to people in the rest of the western hemisphere.

ATTITUDE 1
INDULGING IN
DOUBLE STANDARDS

There are far too many double standards in our society, and this is a luxury we cannot afford. Hypocrisy has become endemic in our attitudes, and proves how confused many of us are. These insincerities result in too much misunderstanding and resentment. Arguing among ourselves seems such a waste of our resources in this increasingly competitive world. There is no other country or terrorist organization that can bring us down, but we certainly can do it to ourselves with these attitudes. There is an old riddle which rings all too true in America today: "I have seen the enemy and he is us."

SOME POPULAR HYPOCRISIES IN AMERICA TODAY

- We value freedom of choice more than almost anything else, yet we demand to be baled out when we realize we've made a bad choice.

- We cherish our freedom of speech, and we defend people's right to burn the flag in the streets and flood the internet with pornography, yet we cannot display the Ten Commandments in a public school or park.

- We demand the government play an ever greater role in our lives, yet we condemn its runaway cost and inefficiency.

- We despise paying taxes and try to minimize our contribution by using every loophole we can find, yet we want government to take on more responsibilities.

- We encourage ambition and generally measure success by how high we've climbed up the economic ladder, yet our tax structure penalizes those who succeed.

- We are a democratic republic in which the will of the majority rules, yet we often abandon majority wishes in our zeal to protect minority wishes.

- We are proud of our electoral process, yet half of us spend the next four years trashing the government because our party lost.

- We love to criticize and demean our politicians, yet we don't find this insulting to the majority of our fellow Americans who voted for them.

- We consider ourselves to be generous and compassionate, yet we prefer the government to decide how much each of us should give and just deduct these involuntary donations from our paychecks.

- We pass more and more laws, yet fewer and fewer people can decipher them.

- We have become more and more litigious, yet we seem to have less and less common sense.

- We allow political correctness to define our public dialog, yet we frequently voice very different opinions in private conversations.

- We preach the benefits of diverse public schools, yet most people would rather send their kids to exclusive private schools if they could afford to.

- We say our diversity is our strength, yet to raise our kids we move into secluded communities where the other people are like us.

- We move into neighborhoods where we hope the people are like us, yet we hardly get to know them because we live such private and busy lives.

- We love to take risks in Las Vegas and on Wall Street, yet we require warning labels on can openers and nail clippers.

- We risk a lot by our dependence on foreign energy, yet we have just about given up drilling for oil and building nuclear power stations for fear of the risks.

- We grumble about our trade imbalance and the loss of manufacturing jobs, yet we scramble to purchase imported products.

- We strike for higher wages and benefits, yet we buy products made by the cheapest labor.

- We love to blame someone for any accident, yet we don't consider that the cost of insurance raises prices for everyone.

- We love to sue big corporations when we feel mistreated, yet we don't consider that the employees, stockholders and consumers will be the ones to pay.

- We claim ethnic background is irrelevant and we prohibit any discrimination on this basis, yet we constantly label people by their ethnicity and require them to identify their ethnic origin on the census forms.

- We say repeatedly that ethnicity, gender, age, religion, etc. are not to be considered, yet we conduct exit polls to determine how each segment of the population votes.

- We claim everyone is equal under the law, yet we devise quotas for certain groups to bypass the competition.

- We diligently screen visitors entering through our airports for links to terrorism, yet we maintain a wide open border thousands of miles long.

- We permit illegal immigrants to work here, yet we pay unemployment benefits to jobless citizens.

- We abhor the idea of people ignoring the rules and living here illegally, yet we excuse them because we like their cheap labor rates and label them as simply "undocumented".

- We judge an 18 year old to be mature enough to vote, wage war, seek an abortion and be sentenced to death, yet not to drink a beer.

- We restrict tobacco use for health reasons, yet we are unable to control the enormous illicit trade in deadly narcotics.

- We cherish the right to life, yet we deny people the right to die when they wish to.

- We deplore the media bias, yet we admit they are extremely influential in forming public opinion.

POLITICAL CORRECTNESS

There is so much that's phony and intellectually dishonest about "political correctness", and many people who subscribe to this philosophy in public hold very different views in private. If we cannot be sincere with ourselves and with each other in public, do we really enjoy freedom of speech? We have swung the pendulum so far in our efforts to avoid offending any particular group that we have long since abandoned all common sense and logic.

While our society becomes more diverse in so many ways, we pretend to take on a generic personality because we are afraid to call things what they are. To be "correct" a Christmas party must be a generic holiday party—though it is never held in January or June. Even though over 70% of the population regard themselves as Christian, you never know when a non-Christian could be offended if you wish him or her Merry

Christmas. What about if he or she has to work over the Christmas break and is offended by your wishing him or her Happy Holidays? Perhaps we should abandon Thanksgiving since this ritual certainly has religious origins and I'm sure one could find a few atheists who take offense to it.

We have become conditioned to speaking in riddles because to talk plainly will inevitably offend someone. Over-sensitivity seems to be our trademark, but we shroud it under the umbrella of "civil liberties". If I want to, I can take offense at just about anything. I am bald, but I may be sensitive about this so you had better not let me know that you've noticed my hair has fallen out. If I apply for a job and you don't hire me I might think you don't like bald people and are prejudiced against me. I might find a clever lawyer to file a discrimination suit. Then you'll see who pays!

If being so sensitive would really make us a more consider-ate society, who could argue against it? Unfortunately, I see little evidence of this, and instead abundant evidence that we are more selfish, crass, impatient and confrontational. Worse, we spend an awful lot of time and energy squabbling over who has more right to be offended. If one can claim any "minority" status, one automatically qualifies for a right to be easily offended. A lot of the time we seem to talk past each other rather than to each other. Forcing people to respect one another seems to have the opposite effect. How can we claim that diversity is an asset when we constantly argue over our differences? Our differences can only be an asset if we use them to complement each other, not to separate us.

DOUBLE-BARRELED CITIZENSHIP

Why is it more "correct" to refer to someone as an African-American or Hispanic-American rather than an American, when our laws prohibit any distinction based on ethnicity? If we were honest with ourselves we would see this for what it is—condescending and patronizing. The term is really a poorly concealed insult. The common argument is that such a person needs some special treatment because he is different, but the real implication is that he is inferior. Which part of the phrase "ethnic origin is irrelevant" is hard to understand, I wonder, and why do we keep referring to ethnicity in countless demographic studies? No citizen should be regarded as anything other than American.

To continue these distinctions merely perpetuates the racial divisions, and implies that these people are something less than full Americans. Indeed, those very people who are given hyphenated labels should take offense at being called anything other than American. It really should be libelous to call anyone a "blank blank"-American. The government must regard everyone as equal—there can be no distinctions and certainly no official preferences. There can be no quotas or affirmative action for "minority" members to bypass the system. No form should ask a person's ethnicity, unless that person is not a citizen.

Even Native-American is a term that has far outlived its relevance. It is not important anymore how we came here, as long as it was legally. It also doesn't matter anymore how many generations we've been here. Whether we have been here for 10,000 years or were naturalized last week, we are all Americans. Some migrated here from Asia by foot across an ice bridge, some came as slaves in rat-infested sailing ships, and some traveled first class.

We have become obsessed with minority labeling, going way beyond ethnic distinctions. We have developed labels for behavioral and ideological patterns, such as Gay-Americans or Pro-life-Americans. The rationale is that by assigning a label to a particular group of people, they gain recognition and credibility. What about all the other labels we could use to distinguish ourselves from each other?

How many levels of minority labeling should there be anyway? How about this one:

1. African-American

2. White-African-American

3. Anglican-White-African-American

4. Married-Anglican-White-African-American

5. Bald-Married-Anglican-White-African-American

It starts to look ridiculous, as indeed it is. This person would appear to be in a very small minority group and should be entitled to every type of benefit imaginable. Coincidently, the above label happens to be my personal favorite since I am definitely of British descent, was born in Africa and became a naturalized American.

QUOTAS

There is nothing democratic or compassionate about setting quotas for "minorities". The implication is that the people included in the quota could not make it in a fair competition. This is patronizing, and those included in any quota should be offended. Only a lack of self esteem could explain why such a person would not be offended. No one deserves a free ride, and there are no free seats available anyhow.

Who exactly determines the definition of a minority group? Any one of us could form a minority group if we wanted to. Minority is a term that should be used for opinions, and particularly for elections. A losing candidate evidently appealed to a minority of the voters. A minority of people agree with quotas or affirmative action.

Whenever a perceived victim of anything is classified as a "minority" it seems acceptable for him to claim discrimination or even racism, and then the rest of us accede to his every demand lest we be accused of bigotry. However, a victim from a non-minority (read: majority) group is expected to take care of himself. The message here is that the poor minority chap cannot fend for himself, which should be considered an insult. Why does he not find this preferential treatment offensive?

Descendants of slaves need to accept that slavery was a worldwide phenomenon for millennia, and is still found in parts of the world. Those selling the slaves were themselves African, and this country was only one of many markets for the slave traders. Indeed, a small percentage of Africans enslaved abroad were brought to this country and most came here while the country was still controlled by foreign powers. There is no American alive today who played any role in that trade. None of us can assume any responsibility for what happened during that era, so we should feel neither shame nor guilt. Whether our ancestors came here voluntarily or not makes no difference to our status as Americans.

DISCRIMINATION

Having a choice is one of our most valued rights, and whenever we choose we discriminate. This word should not carry hostile connotations—it simply means making a choice, or having a preference. Choosing in favor of one person or one philosophy inevitably means not choosing another. If that's prejudice, so be it. Sometimes we have logical reasons for preferring one person or one idea, and sometimes it's just a gut feeling. Not choosing a person doesn't necessarily mean we don't like that person—it just means we have a preference for another. The right to choose means nothing if we don't have the right to prefer.

An employer has the right to choose anyone he wants to work for him, including the right to choose an incompetent person. To tell him he doesn't have the right to choose anyone he wants is ridiculous, because he certainly has the right to choose no one at all. Indeed he has the right to close his business and lay off everyone. He doesn't have to employ any bald people if he doesn't want to, but he can employ only bald ones if he likes.

Not offering someone a job is no different from excluding him from a birthday party. It does not mean there is anything wrong with him, but it does mean that he is not preferred as a friend or as an employee. For him to take offense is ridiculous, and for others to take offense on his behalf is even worse.

Many company managers will tell you that the employees are their biggest asset, but also their biggest liability and, definitely, their biggest headache. Our society should celebrate when anyone is employed, not make it so cumbersome that employers will look for every way to avoid hiring people. Having a job is a privilege, not a right.

Every employee certainly does have rights, including the right to leave the company. Should the employer feel offended and discriminated against when an employee leaves and joins another company? In reality the employer and the employees are mutually dependent, but the employer is the one creating the jobs and our system needs his contribution the most.

APOLOGIZING FOR SUCCESS

Why is it that America became the most successful country, with an economic engine driving almost 40% of the world economy at one time, when we never had more than 5% of the world's population? We certainly didn't have the smartest people in the world, the best educated or the most diligent. Neither did we have a monopoly on natural resources. What we had was a system that encouraged personal achievement and personal responsibility. Almost every other country imposed obstacles to these in the form of government or dictatorial control—some more and some less. Those with more central control have generally fared the worst, and have certainly been the most corrupt.

Success means we can afford to be generous, but not arrogant. Since when is success something to apologize for? We should be proud to be Americans and not ashamed to be the most prosperous country. If we are ashamed of it, we will lose it. Our economy is currently around 20% of world total (depending on the method of measurement), and falling in relative terms. How proud will we be when we reach the 5% mark?

Along with educators, entrepreneurs and employers in general should be among the most highly regarded people in our society, but should also be held to the highest ethical standards. They create jobs, and our system depends on this. We provide enormous incentives to attract employers to our city or state. The more people they promise to employ, the more valuable is their contribution to our society. Along with the jobs come the people, who buy things and pay taxes. Along with the entrepreneurs we need investors who are willing to take risks—calculated risks.

Some people hold the notion that a successful businessman is a greedy villain and should be taxed handsomely. What's so special about him, they say? He's no better than anyone else. He doesn't deserve all that wealth. What's special about him is that he has not abdicated his spirit of freedom, his optimism and his willingness to assume risk. It's thanks to him that the system has any chance of working. He has nothing to apologize for, and we need more like him—as long as he stays honest and displays a high degree of integrity and self-restraint. The key word here is "honest", because those who are not honest deserve to be prosecuted heavily.

To imply that the businessman is abusing the system and exploiting the little guy is totally off base, and very Un-American. The ones abusing the system are trying to push their own agendas and won't admit that most of the time we all end up paying the price. These people are in court suing the company for selling potato peelers without sufficient warning labels about the risks of injury. They are suing the company for not hiring them. They are drawing unemployment checks, welfare checks and food stamps. They are on strike for higher wages and lifetime health coverage, while protesting outside the corporate offices for eliminating 10,000 jobs and outsourcing to China. They are shopping at Wal-Mart for cheap Chinese goods, or else buying expensive European cars. They are on Capitol Hill lobbying the politicians to increase the minimum wage, while complaining about rising costs. They are in court suing the hospital for failure to continue the life support for the 88 year old with terminal cancer, while also demonstrating because their health care premiums have gone up 20% this year to cover the malpractice insurance. They are demonstrating outside the World Bank because loans to developing countries have strings attached, while also demanding we forgive the loans to Africa that ended up in the dictators' Swiss bank accounts. They are holding a sit-in on campus to express their horror that some jailed terrorists or mass murderers were not read their Miranda rights correctly.

ATTITUDE 2
DEMANDING TOO
MUCH FROM
GOVERNMENT

Most of us would never dream of asking our neighbors, much less command them, to do many of the things we expect our government to do. Yet "Government" is nothing more than a convenient word for "all you other Americans who earn anything or buy anything and pay any income tax, sales tax, real estate tax, property tax, estate tax, excise tax, social security tax, Medicare tax, Medicaid tax, gasoline tax, capital gains tax or whatever other taxes and licenses we pay". Whenever we buy anything we pay tax.

We all fund the government, but we tend to forget that the government is US—not THEM. It's WE, the people, not those politicians and bureaucrats, who should be calling the shots. Our elected representatives and the people they hire have a very simple mandate—to execute the wishes of the majority. If the majority wishes are stupid or unreasonable, we will end up with a stupid or unreasonable society. Fortunately I have more confidence in the American people.

Does the U.S. Government reflect the American people? The answer is NO too much of the time. This is not so much the government's fault as it is ours. We have allowed the government to out-grow itself, and it has reached the point where no one can control it. It seems that politicians, by definition, are destined to spend a major part of their time and energy jockeying for power and position, and relegating the affairs of the nation to a secondary role. Far too much of our money is spent on partisan squabbling, with endless plotting, strategizing and investigations just to embarrass and discredit the opponents in order to gain a political edge. Our government is too full of its own importance and too self-serving. No democratic government has ever been as big, as expensive or as unwieldy as this. We have to get a grip on it, and the only way to do this is to limit its size. The most effective way to do this is to limit its budget.

THE ROLE OF GOVERNMENT

I believe much of the disagreement between Americans today arises from our different views on the role of government. At one end of the spectrum are those who think the government should be involved in all aspects of our life and regulate as much as possible. At the other end are those who think the government should be involved to a very limited extent, and that we should retain control over most aspects of our lives.

Many people in the first group are not succeeding very well in life and think that their misfortune is due to unfair laws and practices. They usually have low self esteem and little self confidence. They believe in sharing the wealth, since they stand to gain more than they will contribute. They believe taxes and regulation will level the playing field and allow them to compete and succeed. Since everyone is equal, shouldn't we all have equal wealth? Sounds rather like socialism to me!

This group also includes many elitists who evidently feel somewhat apologetic for their own success, and believe the world is indeed an unfair place. The "less fortunate" among us need a helping hand and, since most people cannot be trusted to divest themselves of the burden of wealth, the government is obviously the most efficient mechanism for achieving this. Sounds a bit too patronizing for my liking!

People at the opposite end of the spectrum tend to be achievers. They value their independence and don't expect any favors. They believe they have to make it on their own, and very often do rise to the top of the pyramid. I doubt there are many entrepreneurs who think the government should increase regulation—they would be happy for the government to get out of their way. We need more entrepreneurs since they create jobs and make our economic system work.

The more we demand from government, the more we can expect two things: it will consume more of our money and it will grow into a dysfunctional, bureaucratic behemoth. Indeed, we've already passed that milestone some time ago, by most standards. The larger the government, the more removed it becomes from representing the individual. We should expect it to become less and less efficient, more and more corrupt, less and less able to react quickly to a crisis; and the return on our investment will be lower and lower.

Government is not an omnipotent power with the answer to all questions. Indeed, government has the answer to very few questions. We should define the questions we want government to find answers for, and keep the list short. We, the people, have the ability to find solutions to our problems. When we buy shares in a corporation we don't expect that corporation to solve all our problems. We buy shares because we believe there are certain things that company does well—they make a good product or provide a good service. They cannot be all things to all people, and neither can the government.

Politicians naturally have a vested interest in expanding the role of government. Their importance and stature increase proportionally with the size of government. We must not let them cajole us into believing they know what's best for us in all situations. Politicians are certainly not endowed with inherently superior powers of reasoning.

We Americans, more than most people on this earth, should understand the significance of the profit motive. Without this motive, most people will not perform at their full potential. Government employees do not have a profit motive, and we should not expect them to be highly efficient or highly productive. The more layers of bureaucracy we build into our government system, the less efficient it will be.

It's we, the people, who decide the role of government; not the politicians who decide what's best for us and how much it will cost us. The people, not the government, create wealth. The government is nothing unless we give it some of our wealth to organize certain aspects of our society. We, the people, have a lot more power than we realize, but we have lost sight of this. We have the power of the purse, which is perhaps all the power we need. We also have the power of the vote, so we can dismiss any representative who doesn't do what we want. The government cannot do anything without our money and our vote, and we need to learn how to use these tools effectively.

COLLECTIVE RESPONSIBILITIES

When we want something from the government, we first have to agree among ourselves that this is a collective responsibility, and then we have to agree to what level we will fund it. "Collective" has several levels—neighborhood, local, state, federal. Most issues in the traditional American life are not collective responsibilities, and those that are can usually be defined as local issues. If any group wants to use its local government to organize something, it's their prerogative. The federal government cannot be in the business of providing benefits to specific groups of people. The criterion should be: is this the responsibility of the majority and will the majority derive the benefit?

Whenever the government pays out compensation to any group, they are in fact taking money from the rest of us. Unless the majority of us have agreed that this is a collective responsibility, no single group has a right to take money from the rest. When we have not agreed that it constitutes a collective responsibility, the government must stay out. There are many channels available to anyone who wants to contribute to a cause, but that is not the role of government. People trying to win favors from government are doing the rest of us a disservice, and the politicians should tell them to go away. Professional lobbyists never represent the majority and should be kept at arms length. Unfortunately these people all too often use smooth talking and bribery to win support for some legislation that benefits their clients.

America was founded on individual freedoms, and the more we veer towards collective responsibility the more we surrender the freedom to make our own personal decisions. Unfortunately many people fail to recognize that we cannot have it both ways. We want our freedoms when it suits us, but the moment anything unexpected happens we want it to be a collective responsibility to put it right. This is a feeble and ignorant attitude. The freedom to make choices MUST be accompanied by the willingness to assume the consequences. Freedom means authority, and authority carries responsibility, as anyone in business knows. One without the other simply does not work. It is hypocritical, unrealistic, unfair and definitely Un-American to believe otherwise.

Whenever we define an issue as a collective responsibility we are admitting that our individual contribution is minuscule. It follows that we also accept that our individual benefit will be minuscule. Collective responsibilities must carry collective benefits. Conversely, individual or group benefits must be paid for by those beneficiaries, and the responsibility assumed by them. What is moral about expecting others to share the cost of anything but not share in the benefits?

Some will argue that those who don't want to share the burden are being selfish, but it is selfish to expect others to share the burden without a payoff. Selfishness is a moral issue and not a legislative one. Most Americans are quite unselfish, and the many charities can testify to this. Unfortunately this unselfishness sometimes warps into naiveté, and the selfish ones try to take advantage of the unselfish ones. We all would love to have an advantage, since we live in a very competitive environment. This means there are literally millions of competing ideas, but many of them are not beneficial to the majority.

We elect representatives and they hire some of us to perform our collective wishes. We should not give these representatives a blank check and we should not expect them to do anything we haven't told them to do and haven't funded. We should seldom be unhappy when the government fails to take action, because we want them to wait for our authorization.

Whenever anyone of us stands up to demand more action from the government, the rest of us should say, "Wait just a minute! If you want us to pay for this, the first thing you can do is quit demanding, and the next thing is explain why it is our collective responsibility, and how we will collectively benefit."

Issues can be collective responsibilities when they are not related to individual choice, such as defense against foreign aggression and protection of our borders. Construction and maintenance of public roads, airports and ports probably are. The government should set the standard for certain things, where our whole country should act in unison and avoid a "free-for-all". Some of these could be certain safety standards, pollution standards, communication standards, quality of drinking water. While the government should establish standards for education and health, it cannot legislate that everyone shall be well educated or super healthy—these depend entirely on the individual.

SOCIAL PROGRAMS

Social programs are charity programs in disguise. It may be our moral responsibility to help another less fortunate person, but no one, including the government, has the right to tell us we have to. If we want to donate funds to some cause or some segment of society, we will do it voluntarily and not be told we have no choice. If we want the government bureaucrats to organize these efforts we will instruct them to. Otherwise, they must stay away.

Accepting the concept that the government will decide who gives help and who receives help takes away the individual choice of helping and breeds selfishness. Those being helped learn to expect this and soon start demanding it, and those helping involuntarily begin to resent it or to feel they are already meeting their moral obligations and that no further action is required.

Handouts have never propelled anyone out of poverty. Only jobs can do that. No one should accept handouts he has not earned, unless he is experiencing a temporary crisis in his life. Continuing reliance on others will destroy self esteem. Only the dignity of working and earning one's living honestly will have a lasting impact on self worth. That businessman may be a greedy multi-millionaire but, by creating jobs, he is doing much more for the "little guy" than any politician can do with taxpayer handouts.

TAXES

The government needs tax money to pay for those benefits we regard as communal responsibilities. I yearn for the day when we can agree that our government will have a budget no larger than $$$$—say 10% of GDP for the federal coffers and another 10% for state and local coffers. With these funds we expect our elected representatives to do the best they can within a defined list of responsibilities. We'll take care of the rest by ourselves, or through voluntary organizations like charities, churches, neighborhood associations and clubs. We expect government to run a tight and efficient operation, and we want a full accounting of revenue and expenditures on a regular basis. Government is forbidden to meddle in any other affairs, and especially forbidden to spend any more money without our approval.

The government should not attempt to redistribute the wealth. There is nothing moral about <u>taking</u> money from one person and handing it to another, regardless of their relative economic standing, and regardless of how they acquired that wealth—as long as it was not by fraudulent means. There is, of course, plenty that's moral about a rich person <u>giving</u> to a poor person. The operative word here is "giving" rather than "taking".

Taxes should not be paid according to one's ability to pay, as this discourages people from maximizing their earnings and motivates them to find every conceivable loophole. The current tax code is so incredibly complicated that loopholes are countless for those who can afford to hire professional tax accountants and lawyers. Sales tax is the only fair method, because one has control over what one buys, one cannot conceal what one buys, and one has every incentive to maximize one's earnings and so afford to buy more. In buying more, one will not only be paying more tax but will also help keep someone else employed.

The traditional American model encourages people to earn their way up the economic ladder. The model also encourages people to share their good fortune with others still struggling their way up the ladder. When we delegate these ideas to the government we destroy the American model. When we take from, sorry I meant tax, those near the top and give it to those near the bottom, sorry I meant those less fortunate through no fault of their own, what incentive is there for anyone to keep climbing?

Anyone who buys anything pays tax. However, it is normally only the income tax portion that gets the attention. Those not paying income taxes naturally hate the idea of tax cuts because these have been characterized as a break for the rich at the expense of the poor. When people talk about tax breaks, by definition only those who pay taxes can get a break.

Don't be tricked by hidden taxes—we, the people, pay all taxes, even when we don't realize we are paying. There is nobody else paying, that's for certain. Corporate income tax, unemployment tax, and taxes that most of us never think about are all passed on to us, the people, in the form of higher prices.

Too many people think the government does not include them, and will attempt to get as much as they can for themselves from government, believing that it is free of charge. Whenever anyone tries to take advantage of the government, they are essentially taking advantage of the rest of us. If they tried that same stunt on any one of us individuals, we would resist strongly, but when the government is involved most of us make the mistake of thinking that someone else is paying the bill.

Tax revenues increase as more people are put to work, because taxes are paid whenever a person earns money or spends money. It follows, then, that with an improving economy there will be more people working, more tax revenue and more funds available for the government. Increasing the tax rate provides only a temporary boost to government revenue, and the long term effect is to slow down the economy and thereby generate less revenue.

DEFICITS

Since the government does not create wealth, any borrowed money must be repaid by future taxpayers. There is very little that's moral about passing this burden along, so we should not lend money to the government, except under extraordinary circumstances. During any pre-defined fiscal period, the government should be prohibited from spending more than we are willing to pay in taxes. Some countries have adopted five-year plans. We must be prepared to pay our own way, and the government should not carry over any debt from one fiscal cycle to the next. Budget deficits should not be permitted.

If we agree that the government needs extra money for some special purpose, we must be willing to pay higher taxes, effective immediately. Probably the simplest and quickest method would be to increase sales tax for the duration of the project. Once the situation is under control, the tax rate should revert to its previous level. Paying back money over extended periods shields us from the reality, and most people lose track of where the money went. We might not be so willing to authorize the added expenditure if we had to "pay-as-we-go". We have accumulated a collective debt equal to almost three-quarters of our GDP, with no sign of reducing this.

We should not give our money to the government for safe-keeping either, because it is not an investment bank. Neither is the government a savings bank and we should not entrust it with our retirement savings. Social Security is a government liability—in other words, a liability for future workers. Is it moral to make commitments on behalf of future generations?

ATTITUDE 3
ASKING TOO LITTLE
OF OURSELVES

This country was founded by people who wanted the freedom to make decisions—good ones and bad ones. If they made good choices, they wanted the rewards that followed. If they made bad choices, they assumed the consequences that followed.

They were eager to participate in the system and take ownership of the government. They wrote safeguards into the constitution so that government could not control their lives. Many of them had fled from places where the government exercised enormous control.

RELINQUISHING PERSONAL RESPONSIBILITY

Apparently there are many of us who are not comfortable making some of our own decisions. Evidently we have lost the desire to take care of ourselves and we want to assign this responsibility to others—usually our company, our labor union, our local government or the federal government. If they send us a monthly bill, so be it. We'll just figure that into our budget along with our mortgage payment, car payment and credit card bills. Hopefully they will make it painless for us by taking the money before we even see it. With any luck, mind you, we won't have to pay those bills at all, or we will get a refund—someone else with greater "means" will sponsor us. Yeah, make those fat cats pay their fair share of the taxes!

With more people adopting the attitude that they have a right to a decent living, to a minimum wage, to lifetime health care, to a smoke-free environment, and even a risk-free environment, it follows that someone else has to guarantee those rights. Those who want the government to do more for them are generally not the ones who contribute the most in taxes. They are the ones who complain the most when the government is slow to respond to their needs. They want a "nanny" state, but don't admit that this is the antithesis of how America became strong in the first place.

When we constantly look elsewhere for someone to carry our burden, it seldom brings out the best in us. It seems strange that so many of us constantly look towards the government to make decisions that we could, and should, make ourselves. Apparently we would rather have the politicians pass regulations so that we avoid the tough decisions. We should not wait for the government to take a leading role in our lives. Indeed, we should not want it to.

OWNERSHIP IN GOVERNMENT

We are all shareholders in the government—Uncle Sam Incorporated. Everyone has one share. No one owns more than anyone else, even though we contribute vastly different amounts. No one should wield more power than anyone else nor have any right to special privileges. An election is a shareholders' meeting, where we all get the opportunity to choose the management and board of directors. While we don't expect to make money from our investment, we do expect a return in many other ways. The returns are not proportional to our investments, and those who pay the highest dues should not expect the highest returns, but neither should those who pay the lowest dues. Ironically, those who pay the least usually demand that government do the most.

You may be a passive owner, or even an unwilling owner, but you still own part of the government and you pay your membership dues every time you buy anything. Even if we do think it's a bad investment, we cannot sell our stake in the government. Some people think they can sell out by not participating, or not voting. Other people think that because they voted for the other party it's okay to trash the government in office. When we criticize our government we are essentially insulting the intelligence and judgment of those around us who voted for those representatives. We should use persuasive arguments and constructive criticism to try to convince as many voters as possible to alter their point of view before the next election.

Since we own the government, we must demand a very high standard of integrity and ethical behavior from our elected representatives. We must not excuse them for lapses in judgment on this score. They are privileged to be representing America in the eyes of the world, and we will be judged by how they perform and behave. For the American model to function, we are obligated to replace any representative who does not perform to the highest standards. Incompetence at any level should never be tolerated. Corruption and handing out favors to select groups should be cause for immediate dismissal.

Conversely, however, we should compensate our representatives well because we want to attract the best candidates. Politics requires very strong characters because it is an extremely challenging profession. No matter how the politicians decide on any given issue, some of us will be unhappy. So long as we believe they have tried to act in the best interests of the majority, we should support them.

CHARITY

Americans are traditionally very generous and compassionate people, and help for the victims of a disaster will be forthcoming—indeed, 1 billion dollars or more was donated to charity after the devastation following hurricane Katrina in the summer of 2005, not to mention the countless hours of volunteering. However, the government was quick, though not quick enough for some, to authorize over $60 billion, with more installments to follow.

If the government is to assume the role of baling out the victims and give so generously on our behalf, I can't help wondering why we bother to give such insignificant amounts to the charitable organizations. What can the charities do with a meager 1 billion—probably just get in the way of the government, right! With Uncle Sam playing the role of "Mr. Generosity" I guess we don't need charities. Let's just choose the most efficient method of donating, and stick to that. If Uncle Sam is most qualified to handle this, let's do it his way. The government will tell us how much we each owe. It will be easy to appear charitable—all we have to do is write a check to the IRS. Anyone who wants to contribute more can certainly write an extra check, or perhaps take advantage of fewer tax loopholes next April.

Of course, this has the added advantage of removing the burden of responsibility from our shoulders. We also have an easy scapegoat when the money is not well spent. The real test of our generosity toward our fellow Americans is how much we would give to charity if the government could not appropriate our money. How charitable is it to donate when someone tells you how much you must give? How logical is it to have charitable donations tax deductible? If someone wants to give $100, let them give $100, not $70 and then have the rest of us cough up the other $30.

By abdicating our social responsibilities to the government, we, the people, have a tendency to think we are fulfilling our obligations through our taxes and that it is not necessary to do any more. Get the government out of the charity business and let's see how charitable we really are. We may be very pleasantly surprised or we may be horrified. Either way we will finally know the truth.

For the government to usurp this privilege is really an insult to our humanity. We have allowed some elected officials to tell us: "well, we know you are a pretty selfish bunch out there, so we will decide how much each of you should donate to your fellow being." I don't recall anyone thanking those who pay higher taxes for their generosity. I guess that's their obligation since they earn more, right? Since we can't trust them to be generous, we'll just force them to be. Do we want the government to be our referee?

ATTITUDE 4
EXPECTING TOO
MUCH FROM OTHERS

Smart trial lawyers who argue in front of a jury that it is the evil corporate giant who deliberately takes advantage of the poor unsuspecting consumer are playing the old tongue-in-cheek game. Firstly, it is nonsense to argue that the consumer had no choice in the matter. Secondly, the consumer in question should feel insulted to be called unsuspecting, which implies that he is ignorant of the risks involved in buying anything. Thirdly, and most importantly, it is deceitful to imply that the damages paid by the corporation will come out of the CEO's pocket. A corporation is made up of "little people" and it is fellow Americans who end up paying—employees, stockholders and consumers—while a few individual plaintiffs may get rich. Oh, and any money the lawyers make is purely incidental, of course!

LAWSUIT MANIA

Sue for damages whenever we can find another party to blame. Every manufacturing and service company needs liability insurance these days to protect against lawsuits, because the threat of being sued is so prevalent. Insurance companies get rich from this, and they are only too happy to "sell up" the risk. Liability insurance drives up the cost for everyone, since the costs are passed on to the consumer in the form of higher prices.

If I smoke for thirty years and die of lung cancer, obviously I wasn't given sufficient warning of the dangers, and you other smoking taxpayers should compensate my estate with higher taxes and prices. Naturally I sympathize with all those non-smokers who died from lung cancer because they won't get a nickel.

If I demand higher wages and my company out-sources my job, obviously I am a victim of unfair down-sizing by greedy business tycoons. You other working taxpayers should foot my bills until I find another job, in the form of unemployment taxes.

In short, no matter what happens to me that I decide I don't like, I will do my best to find someone to blame. If that culpable party has money, all the better, because then I can sue for damages—the more money they have, the more damages I can claim. I'm sure I can find a lawyer who's only too happy to take my case on a contingency basis. We'll shoot for the moon and make those suckers pay. What better source of cash than all you other taxpayers—uh, sorry, I meant to say the government. Hey, the government wastes so much money anyway, why shouldn't I get a little piece of the action?

While we must leave the door open for damage awards to those people who have a good case, there has to be a reasonable limit on these awards. Making outrageous claims for compensatory damages is very selfish and harmful to our system. Even worse are the punitive awards—supposedly to punish the company—which often run into the multi-multi-millions or billions. Shouldn't the money awarded as a penalty, or fine, be paid into the public coffers anyway, not to the plaintiff? Why should the lawyers take home a percentage of the award?

Should we cherish our corporations as places of employment, or should we vilify them for damaging our environment, for selling unsafe products, for making too much money, for not improving their stock price, for exploiting the little guy, for not paying higher wages, for not hiring enough minorities, for laying off workers, for charging too much, for not paying enough taxes.

Suing a company into bankruptcy only undermines our economic system. We are suing ourselves out of business and out of jobs. If the executives have been dishonest, let's punish them severely. Lawyers and plaintiffs generally don't like that idea because the executives' pockets aren't nearly as deep as the corporation's. These executives should not be able to hide behind the corporate screen.

THE TRICKLE-DOWN EFFECT

Here is a typical sequence of events:

1. These damage awards become corporate liabilities and are passed on as price increases to its customers. Consumers, then, are the first tier of those paying the bill.

2. The corporation may indeed suffer a fall in market share as a result of the higher prices, and the next phase requires cutting costs, which very often translates into cutting jobs. Those laid-off workers, i.e. fellow Americans, constitute the second tier of those paying the bill.

3. The next phase includes out-sourcing those jobs to low cost areas, usually in third world countries.

4. The final phase is closing the business completely, moving it off shore, and laying off all the workers.

5. If sales drop and the company doesn't cut costs fast enough, the stockholders will see the value of their investments fall, which for many folks may be their retirement savings. Many people holding mutual funds probably didn't even know they owned stock in that company. Those ordinary citizens are the third tier of bill payers.

6. I wonder how the jury feels once they realize what happened after they awarded those huge damage penalties—who exactly were they trying to penalize anyway? Hopefully not the "little people" described above.

7. No doubt the plaintiff prefers not to ponder that question too much, and may even convince himself that justice was done.

8. The trial lawyers from both sides will be contemplating their strategy for the next case as they head down to the bank to count their winnings.

9. The rest of us will read in the papers that another company laid off umpteen thousand workers, and we'll turn the page. So what else is new!

10. We'll read on the next page that the trade imbalance hit another record last month with imports outpacing exports by $60 billion. That doesn't sound terribly encouraging but, oh well, thank goodness it doesn't affect me!

11. Then we'll head off downtown in our Swedish car to buy a new TV from China, some shoes from Brazil and perhaps a tailored suit from India.

12. Wow, isn't it fun having all these choices, and good prices too? Too bad we won't have our jobs much longer!

TOBACCO INDUSTRY EXAMPLE

The tirade against the tobacco industry is perhaps the most obvious example of expecting others to compensate us, and the most blatant abuse of our justice system. The whole premise is absurd that a person who died from lung cancer after smoking for 30 years is not responsible and someone else is to blame. It is more than absurd—it is a deceitful lie, an insult to that person's intelligence and a distortion of our constitutional right to make free choices.

What is the meaning of freedom if not to make our own choices—good ones and bad ones? To argue that the individual bears no responsibility for his choices is ridiculous, dangerous and indicative of a feeble mindset. It implies he is not free—that someone else is responsible for his decisions.

If we accept the notion that individuals are too stupid or too ignorant to make personal choices, then our days as a superpower society definitely are numbered. Most of us make stupid choices sometimes, and that's our prerogative. Mistakes have a price, and we must be willing to pay the price for our own mistakes. A poor choice is a mistake, and smoking for 30 years is a poor choice.

The proponents of the anti-smoking campaign hide behind the smoke screen (no pun intended) of saving lives. Who gave them the job of saving our lives? I think each of us prefers to live our own life as we choose. Do we want some self-appointed "nanny" saving ourselves from ourselves? Besides, no one lives forever, so what exactly do we mean by saving a life? All we can possibly do is prolong our lives a few more years, perhaps. Will someone else want to save us again in a few years' time?

When that argument no longer flies very well, the anti-smoking lobby contends that it costs us all money to pay for the health care of these smokers. Smokers statistically carry an increased risk factor, and they already pay higher health and life insurance premiums. Let the insurance companies charge them more if necessary. That's also the price of a bad choice. The cost of smoking is very high, but smokers still have the right to make that bad decision. To claim that the company is responsible because of inadequate warnings is absurd, insulting and Un-American.

Yet a third argument implies that some people are allergic to second-hand smoke. While this may be true, how far do we carry the idea that if I find another person's habit irritating he should quit doing it? If this is the standard, there are many other habits we should not tolerate. Besides, it's my choice whether or not to frequent a restaurant where smoking is permitted.

With all the fuzzy logic spewed forth in this debate, the real truth has been totally lost; and deliberately so. The tirade against the industry has everything to do with money for the lawyers and the government, and very little to do with people's health. If the product is really so dangerous, it should be illegal anyway. Judging by past experience and the multi-billion dollar narcotics industry, prohibition may not reduce consumption by much. Worse than this, though, prohibition would mean no more companies to sue and no more tax money coming in. No wonder the lawyers and politicians don't like that idea! The tax on cigarettes could also be increased to the point where very few people could afford to smoke, but then the contraband market would take over and the tax revenue would dry up. Taxes can be self-defeating.

DRUG COMPANY EXAMPLE

Unlike the above example where virtually everyone agrees that smoking is unhealthy, consider a pharmaceutical company that develops a new drug. Years of research and many millions of dollars in studies are required before it gets approved by the FDA. What is the meaning of approval if there is no waiver of responsibility for the safety of the drug? Conversely, let's waive the approval process and hold the company fully accountable for the drug's safety. No one can guarantee there is zero risk associated with this drug. If we want zero risk, the drug will never get to market.

The cost of this approval process is paid by the users of the drug. (Actually most of us help pay through our insurance plans, whether or not we use the drug.) These users are fellow Americans, and they are willing to pay the price if their doctor convinces them that the drug has a good chance of helping them. Be happy that some smart scientists developed this drug, and be willing to accept the risk. Not willing to accept the risk? Don't buy the drug!

But in America can't I eat my cake and still have it? If I decide the drug was wrong for me I'll just sue the manufacturer for selling an unsafe product. Who do I want to pay compensation, you ask? Why, all those fat cats running the company. But if I sue the drug company won't they pass that cost on to all the other people who use their products? Well, I certainly don't want to punish them. And won't insurance premiums increase for us all? And didn't the FDA approve the drug? Well yes, but I guess they didn't do a thorough job of reviewing the study data. Hey, that's a great idea, I'll sue the government. Okay, then we all will pay the price through our taxes. Good, that feels better (and should be more lucrative too)!

If the executives of the drug company were dishonest and withheld information from the FDA, punish them harshly. Make them pay retribution and rot in jail for a few years. If the FDA did not do the best job they could, fire them. Otherwise, bad luck. Nobody deliberately targeted me, and the company was not negligent or deceitful. There was an element of risk and, unfortunately, I happen to be one of those statistics. It's not my fault, but it's not yours either, and why should you owe me any compensation?

ATTITUDE 5
DESIRING RISK-FREE
LIVES

America was settled mostly by people who were willing to take risks—in many cases risking everything they had. Certainly the constitution doesn't guarantee a life free from risk. Surely we are savvy enough to understand that there can be no free choice without risk—we make our choices and we take our chances. The freedom to choose means nothing without the freedom to take a chance at winning, or losing.

Too many people want to remove risk from their lives. We want warning labels on everything—from cigarettes to can openers. We don't want the responsibility of deciding for ourselves if an item carries a risk factor, and so any item without a warning label must be risk-free. Too bad there isn't a warning label on a snort of cocaine or a heroin needle. Even when there is a warning label, we still don't assume the risk ourselves if we think we can find a clever lawyer to take our case.

Even correct use of many products carries a risk factor. If gun ownership were not guaranteed by the constitution there is no doubt that guns would have been outlawed by people who believe them to be too dangerous for the average person to own. The automobile is a pretty risky machine, and every driver would do well to treat it as such. Those manufacturers that build safer cars should expect to see improved sales. The question is how much does a totally safe car cost to build, and how many of us want to pay the price? Some of us would rather pay less and assume a greater risk. How about if we all drive around in tanks, or in cars with a top speed of 10mph? Surely we could "save" approximately 40,000 lives a year in road deaths, but how many of us want to pay the price?

Those wanting a risk-free life also want a life devoid of responsibility. They must also want a life without the satisfaction of achievement. They want a life without the risk of failure. If we are so afraid of failure, we will be afraid of doing much of anything. Failure is not desirable, but it presents an opportunity to show our true character. Trying again and overcoming failure is probably the surest way to earn respect from others and from ourselves. Demanding someone else bale us out earns no respect—least of all self-respect. Some failures are self-inflicted and some are not. In the latter case we will find others are more willing to help, but it is NOT their obligation.

We haven't built a nuclear power station in years because we are afraid of an accident, though it is one of the cleanest forms of energy and statistically very safe. We hardly drill for oil anymore because there could be a spill. What about the risk we take in depending on imported oil from unstable and sometimes unfriendly countries?

America did not climb to the top with people afraid to take a chance. We cannot expect to stay at the top in this competitive world if we are unwilling to take risks.

LAWS FOR EVERYTHING

We should not try to devise a legal system that protects us from all risk. With every additional law with which to govern ourselves we tend to imagine that another risk has been eliminated. Once we accept that every facet of life is governed by a law, it leads us down a slippery slope of irresponsibility. It leads to the dangerous belief that any behavior is acceptable as long as it doesn't contravene a law. Anything becomes acceptable so long as one can get away with it legally. While it is true that everyone is innocent until proven guilty, there are many types of behavior that are wrong even if we cannot prove it in a court of law. Our objective should not be to invent a law to address every conceivable eventuality.

Of course we need laws to prosecute those who try to take care of themselves at the expense of others. The legal system is to protect against abusers. It must protect the rights of the individual, but not at the expense of the community. It is not supposed to protect people from all forms of risk. It is certainly not supposed to protect people from themselves—from their own ignorance or stupidity. It is not supposed to protect the unsuccessful from the successful. It is not supposed to benefit the lawyers and politicians more than anyone.

It is often said that America is a country of laws. That's an understatement, and not necessarily a compliment. It isn't said often enough that we are also a country of lawyers—about two-thirds of all the world's lawyers for 5% of the world's population. The more laws we have, the more lawyers we need. Laws should be written for the common man to understand, and not veiled in ambiguity for the lawyers to interpret in a myriad of ways. The more laws we have, the harder it is for anyone to know what is legal and what isn't, and the less chance we have of enforcing them. We should not measure the success of our legislatures by how many laws they pass while in session. Politicians compete for attention by inventing new bills, but perhaps they would do well to eliminate many of the existing laws.

We expect that passing a law will end the debate and simplify the issue into black and white. Nothing is further from the truth—the law only affords an opportunity for different interpretations and endless discussion. That in turn requires a cumbersome and expensive system of courts to listen to opposing arguments. The losing side won't like the verdict and will file an appeal. There is no incentive to resolve the debate through common sense—that would be far too simple. Much better to camouflage the issue in complexity and fuzzy logic and drag it out! Pretending it is so complicated justifies postponing the decision and allows everyone to feel good about having their opinion heard. Lawyers generally bill by the hour and don't make much money from quick decisions.

EMERGENCIES

An old adage reminds us that "Failure to plan on your part does not constitute an emergency on my part." An emergency is strictly an event that no one could have reasonably predicted or planned for. To what extent does the affected individual or community assume the risk, and when do the rest of us step up to the plate?

A terrorist attack may be considered an emergency, even though it can be argued that it should have been predicted by the intelligence community. Should the government compensate for these things? Should the families of the 9/11 victims have been paid huge sums in compensation? A better case could be made if the victims had been civil servants. Will the government compensate all those affected in time of war, or should we each just write a check to ourselves?

Most people would probably categorize natural disasters as emergencies. A hurricane is not necessarily an emergency, because we know they occur every year in certain parts of the country and we can see them coming several days in advance, thanks to the technology of weather satellites. An earthquake is generally accepted as an emergency, but in reality we know where the high risk areas are, even though we cannot see them coming. A tsunami would be an emergency.

The point here is not so much what defines an emergency, but what types of emergency we consider our collective responsibilities. It's fine for Floridians to agree that hurricanes in that state are their collective responsibility, because the whole state is a high risk area. But is it right that Michigan residents assume part of this risk? They never get hurricanes, though they have to contend with harsh winters that Floridians don't consider their problem.

KATRINA EXAMPLE

Watching the victims crowded into the New Orleans superdome inspired many mixed emotions, but one thought that would not let go: the people that made this country great would have reacted quite differently. They would have admitted they made a bad choice by not evacuating, would probably have been too proud to ask for assistance, would have been extremely grateful for any help offered, and would certainly not have turned that tragedy into a political football.

By contrast, the Katrina victims and their political allies came out swinging—attacking and blaming the government for their plight and demanding immediate rescue. They claimed to be the victims of the hurricane and also victims of discrimination. This is a sure indication that they have surrendered their personal pride and responsibility. Moreover, should the rest of us also be angry at the government for not sending our tax dollars to their assistance quickly enough, or for not spending our money to reinforce the levees thirty years ago? Or maybe because the government didn't organize any drivers for the hundreds of school buses that could have carried the people out of the city? Why was the government so stingy with our tax money, anyway—didn't we give them a blank check years ago? Let's blame the government—we do our share, we pay our taxes, so what more do they want from us? Let's not even consider that blaming the government is implicating ourselves.

It is so easy to blame the government for whatever happens. It absolves us of any liability and indicates that it isn't us who are incompetent. "By Jove, we elected those people to take care of these things and we gave them our tax dollars, so they have no excuse." I wonder what our excuse is!

All of us not directly affected by the hurricane were probably sympathetic towards the victims, but it is pretty hard to remain sympathetic when they start suing us. In their mind they are just suing the government for inefficiency, but we know who the real target is. Since they didn't get their hands on our tax dollars quickly enough, we should pay a penalty. That seems to be the new American way—keep paying more until they promise not to sue us. In the traditional American spirit, we would have told the victims how much we could afford to donate and then wished them good luck.

The 2005 hurricane season seems to have really accentuated the level to which we have descended in self-un-reliance. Is it the role of the government, or should I say the rest of you Americans, to bale me out every time a hurricane destroys my house? If I live below sea level in Louisiana I may be coming back to you every year. I wonder how many times you'll rebuild my house? The last time I checked no one was forcing me to live in a hurricane zone, but that's my choice. If I don't want to assume the risk, I should move. I may move to Buffalo, NY, and then you guys have to shovel me out when we get an extra heavy snowfall. The point is: how far do we carry the idea that it's not my fault so you guys have to help me? It certainly isn't my fault that a hurricane flattened my house, but the risk is still mine to carry. Let's not confuse fault with risk. Too many people not only want a risk-free life, they also want a fault-free one. Just because something isn't my fault does not mean it must be someone else's. I cannot ask, much less demand, that you other Americans compensate me whenever it's not my fault. I don't think it's yours either!

ATTITUDE 6
UNWILLING TO
BALANCE OUR TRADE

It is very satisfying to see other countries improving their living standards, and we hope the whole world can one day eliminate poverty. However, we do not have to give up ground for them to gain ground. The playing field is not level and has no boundaries, and we are not all playing by the same rules anyway.

Communications have improved so dramatically in recent decades that the world has become much more accessible. News and money travel from anywhere to anywhere in milliseconds, while people and goods go anywhere in hours. Easy communications and increased trade have broken down many of the barriers between nations. It's great to trade goods and ideas with all the world's citizens, but we must not trade away our capacity to develop these. We are becoming citizens of the world economy, and need to compete on the world stage.

We have to decide which hat we want to wear on stage, since almost all of us have two hats—our employee hat and our consumer hat. As an employee we hate to compete with all those imports, but as a consumer we love the competition from all those imports. It's an illusion to think we can enjoy eating our cake and keep it indefinitely too. The real challenge is to find the right balance.

UNION MENTALITY

Let's demand ever higher wages, more benefits and job protection! We little people just want a living wage, without over-exerting ourselves. Make the company pay—they've got the money. So what if the company has to raise their prices—that's their problem. So what if the company loses market share and has to cut costs. Just so long as they don't cut our jobs! They should lay off some of those white collar stiffs who earn too much anyway. (Unfortunately some company executives do pad their own wallets so lavishly that one can sympathize with this mentality.)

Labor unions were born in an age when it was not uncommon to find employers mistreating their employees. Unions played a useful role, but those days have long gone. Today the union mentality has morphed into a dangerous concept where the employer owes a job to the employee. This notion completely contradicts the American model. If we regard a job as a right, what incentive is there to perform well? The American worker is in danger of becoming second rate. Unions are a threat to our system and our competitiveness, by driving the cost up and the performance level down. Couple this with the lawsuit mania driving up the cost of doing business, and is it any wonder so many jobs are being driven overseas?

The idea of collective bargaining is for those who fear that they are not competent to negotiate on their own merits. Job protection is for the incompetent. An employer will rarely fire a competent worker, but if he does that's his prerogative. That's the difference between employer and employee. They are mutually dependent, but the employer retains the right to withdraw his offer to buy the services anytime he chooses, and the employee retains the right to withdraw his services at anytime. The competent worker should have little trouble finding employment elsewhere.

Hey, nobody told me that there is a worker in China who can do my job for a fraction of the cost. Or maybe it takes two or three of them to do my job—still at a fraction of the cost. Nobody warned me that my job might be out-sourced to him (or them). Nobody warned me that all our jobs might be out-sourced. Who's going to support my family now—I guess I'll just draw unemployment until it runs out and then, well, maybe I can serve fast food to those who still have their jobs.

A generation or so ago, many companies moved south and west to evade unions and high taxes, and America saw a massive migration of its population. We are witnessing the same happening again, except now it's a lot more serious—the companies don't move to another state, they move to another country. The jobs move away, but the workers don't. The jobs move to where the workers cost less, or they are more willing, or the labor laws are less intrusive and the lawyers less numerous.

IMPORT MANIA

Free trade sounds great, and may the best man win. However, it must be universally adopted if it's to succeed. Unfortunately free trade American-style almost always means free in-coming but not out-going. Most other countries want to protect their home industries by limiting imports with duties and restrictions. This means local industries don't have to compete on the world market, and they become less productive. Local prices are higher than necessary, quality does not measure up to international standards, and consumers have limited choice. On the flip side, though, jobs are less likely to be out-sourced. Some of the reluctance to import is deliberate government policy, but some of it is pure national pride and patriotism on the part of the people.

The traditional American model encourages the widest choice possible, with more competition to keep quality up and prices down. This works well within our borders, and America is recognized as a shoppers' paradise. However, on an international scale it takes on a different meaning. Our appetite for imports seems to be insatiable, and we have been trading in the red for the last 25 years. Our trade imbalance continues to break records month after month. We are now more content than ever to buy what other countries produce, because the items are cheaper (for the most part) or better (in some cases). It is easy to understand why they would be cheaper when coming from a developing country, but we need to consider what we are doing to our own pay scales when we buy these products. It's harder to understand why they would be better—shouldn't we be able to produce the best quality items? "Made in America" used to be a symbol of quality, but we are rapidly losing that reputation.

How long can we continue to import more than we export without the value of our currency falling dramatically or our interest rates increasing? Foreigners and foreign governments have lent trillions of dollars to the U.S. Government, own over half of all our currency in circulation and are buying up our companies. For the time being those foreigners are happy to reinvest in our country, and thus shelter us from the real effect. As soon as this stops we will be in for a rude awakening. They could decide this at any time—for pure business reasons, for political reasons or for hostile reasons. Regardless of their reasons, they could destroy our economy when this happens.

We have gone from being the engine of the world to being marginally self-sufficient. If we lose our self-sufficiency, we lose our independence. If there was a blockade on imports, how would we fare? It sounds cute and trendy to say "well if U.S. manufacturers can't compete, they deserve to go out of business". Let's ship scrap metal to Japan and buy it back as a car or computer for less than it costs to make that item here. We have lost the national pride and patriotism we once had.

We all owe it to ourselves and our families to stretch our budgets as far as we can, and if that means buying cheaper imported products, so be it, we say. We want to earn $30 / hour but we want to buy products made by workers earning $30 / week. At this rate we will buy ourselves out of a job. In the short term it seems like a bargain to buy the imported item for $ instead of the American one for $$$$$. Once we all figure this out, there won't be many of those $30/hr jobs left. Just ask all those thousands of auto workers who soon will be losing their jobs in what were once the world's biggest corporations.

Oh well, you say, many of these foreign companies set up facilities in the U.S. (e.g. Toyota, BMW) so there will be jobs for us. Only, they will be the employers and we the employees—in our own country. They will only do this to the extent that it is cost effective. Once they have unions demanding outrageous wages and benefits, these jobs will disappear again.

Unfortunately it is not only the cheap imports that are swamping our markets. It is also some expensive items that we have lost the ability to make competitively, or have simply fallen behind in technology.

We should put out the word that America is open for fair trade anytime, but we should not bend over backwards to seal trade agreements with every country. The reality is that we can survive on our own better than any other country can, unless, of course, we continue much further on our current path. Everyone wants access to the American market, because we are the largest consumer block in the world. Americans will buy anything. It is ridiculous for countries like Brazil and India to insist that we throw our markets wide open while they maintain some of the most stringent import restrictions—often 50% or more in duties. Indeed, our markets are already the most open. Countries that impose restrictions and duties on our products should expect no less from us.

If we genuinely aspire to become a totally service economy we need to be improving our education system significantly.

We will require the best educated people in the world in order for us all to service the world with new technology breakthroughs and development. Unfortunately, rather than advancing ahead of everyone, our education system is falling behind even many developing countries. Many of our high school graduates are barely literate, and we have a long way to go before all our kids are ready for the challenges of providing high quality service—unless, of course, we want to serve fast food to the rest of the world.

FOREIGN AID

Jobs, jobs, jobs. The most effective way to assist other countries is to foster the conditions that provide them with jobs. We should identify specific countries we want to assist—not with handouts, but by allowing their products into our market with no restrictions. Only in these special cases should we tolerate an uneven playing field. Putting the people in any country to work is the best hope for them to improve their living conditions. For most of these countries their worst enemy is their own government, and we don't need to be sending money to those corrupt governments. History proves that the common people are the last ones to benefit.

Having a job is the only way the people will eventually wield any power over their own government. Buying their products gives everyone something in return. We can stretch our budgets further, while those people have jobs and an income. It is also harder for their governments to get their hands on the money.

As the buyers of those products, we have much of the power. We can refuse to buy anything made by people who earn less than $30 / hour, or we can buy the cheapest product on the market which may be produced by people earning $30 / week. From my observation, most of us are quite happy to buy "el cheapo". We'll just keep buying those products and let the people take care of themselves and their government.

What about those "sweat shops" we hear about in those countries? Isn't it wrong to import products made by those poor, exploited people? Hey, those people are only too happy to have a job, and only too happy that we are willing to buy the fruits of their labor.

Like anything, there is a price to pay, but it is not always obvious who is paying. Our own workers who lose their jobs to the imports are really the ones paying the price for aiding those other countries. Obviously we need to be quite selective about which countries we offer to help.

ATTITUDE 7
ABANDONING
MAJORITY RIGHTS

When we constantly push for minority rights, the rights of the majority inevitably get pushed aside. We should not make it beneficial to claim "minority" status. Diversity can be an asset, but not if we spend valuable time, energy and resources arguing over our differences.

LANGUAGE, RELIGION AND CULTURE

If we permit our language, religion and culture to be diluted, we lose our identity. America is an English-speaking country. This means all official forms should be in English, and all government business conducted in English. We should not be told to press "1" for English, "2" for Spanish or "3" for Chinese. How many choices would we need? This does not mean other languages are disallowed, and indeed we should encourage our kids to learn foreign languages to better conduct business internationally.

America is predominantly a Christian country. This means the majority of people want to practice Christianity and celebrate its holidays. Only Christian holidays and symbols should be sanctioned by the government, though the government will not enforce the practice of any particular religion. Of course people can practice other religions, and the constitution guarantees their right to do so. The First Amendment specifically permits everyone to practice his preferred religion without harassment.

The Ten Commandments is a list of original Judaeo-Christian laws and they embody the principles on which this country was founded. The majority of Americans still embrace them, and the list should be on display wherever practical—especially in public places like schools, public squares and government offices. It seems preposterous that we can waste so much time arguing over whether anyone could be offended by one or more of these rules. Except for the three rules that are incorporated into our criminal code, no one is compelled to adhere to any of them. Adulterers will probably ignore #7, and atheists will no doubt choose to ignore several.

America is a bastion of western civilization. Our laws reflect our western European heritage and we should not devise new laws to accommodate other cultures. This does not mean people cannot practice different styles of culture provided their practices or rituals do not contravene the laws of our western culture.

It has never been easy to describe an American, since America has always been a country where various cultures converged. However, we evolved primarily as a western European culture, and this has definitely served us well. For the last thirty-odd years we have permitted an accelerated dilution of our culture, and it is now impossible to identify an American by any definition. Can our society continue to absorb people with totally different cultures without losing its own identity? Controlling our borders is paramount to protecting our identity.

Some people believe we must aim towards a totally multi-cultural society, with no single culture dominating. These multi-cultural advocates argue that globalization makes this inevitable, and that this in no way implies the demise of the American model. They say America was built by immigrants and diversity has always been our strength. They believe that mixing us all up into a generic blend will dissolve our differences so we will become one happy family. This seems unrealistic and naïve—diversity has been the cause of many of our growth pains. If anything, the more diverse we become the more we seem to find to argue about. History offers precious few examples that suggest a cultural blend makes for a more harmonious society. I want to believe the American model can exist within a multi-cultural society, but it will require a lot more effort to maintain and defend. First and foremost, we must stop calling attention to our differences all the time, and focus instead on what qualities unite us and distinguish us as Americans.

IMMIGRATION

Everyone should fall into one of the following categories, and must be able to prove his/her identity:

- Citizen by Birth—a person born here, with at least one parent a citizen or legal resident at the time of birth.

- Naturalized Citizen—a foreign-born person who became a legal resident first and who subsequently opted to become a citizen through the proper channels.

- Legal Resident—a foreigner living here with a government issued "green card" and normally required to have some special skill or else a relative already living here legally. Enjoys most of the same rights as a citizen—but certainly not voting rights or welfare rights. Can be deported for serious offenses.

- Legal Visitor—a foreigner living here on a temporary holiday or work visa. Must go home when this expires, has limited rights while here, and can be deported for serious offenses.

All others are illegal aliens, NOT "Undocumented-Americans". Illegal aliens and their children have no rights—by definition they should not be here, and must be deported whenever caught. We must not make it easy or attractive for people to come and live here illegally. Referring to them as simply "undocumented" makes light of the fact that they are criminals, thumbing their noses at our laws.

Illegal aliens hide beneath the surface of society, and are a huge potential security risk. They can only survive through crime or by finding willing employers. Employers and anyone assisting illegal aliens must be prosecuted heavily. They too are criminals.

Controlling who comes across our borders is essential if we are to ever stop the narcotics trade. There are so many reasons to protect our borders that one would think we would have implemented an effective strategy years ago. The fact that we have not done so is another example of how inefficiently the government operates. There are so many competing arguments and interests that politicians cannot agree on what action to take. The cost of our inaction is incalculable in terms of lost jobs, lost taxes, health and education services, infrastructure overload, drug trafficking and security risks.

Legal and controlled immigration is great and we want to encourage people with skills. However, so long as we have any unemployment, how many more people do we really need coming into this country who are willing to take jobs that Americans can't get or don't want? The issue is akin to out-sourcing, but instead of out-sourcing to overseas workers the jobs are out-sourced to new immigrants or temporary visitors who are willing to work for less than their American counterparts. One can argue, at least, that it is far preferable to bring the worker here than to send the job off-shore.

ATTITUDE 8 HOOKED ON TOLERANCE

Open-mindedness is to be encouraged, but we don't have to accept every distorted idea. Someone's right to express an idea does not imply an obligation for us all to accept it. We certainly don't want it thrust down our throats in the name of freedom of speech.

Common sense should tell us that certain behaviors are unacceptable. However, the wave of "political correctness" has conditioned us to tolerate any behavior, no matter how bizarre, and we are petrified of being sued if we don't. We have to be very strong to remain steadfast in the onslaught of so much confusion and baloney. What about our majority right to feel offended?

EVERY BEHAVIOR IMAGINABLE

We are subjected to a daily barrage of people flaunting weird behavior, just because they can. Our constitution protects them and we are scared to oppose their ideas. Our excessive number of laws implies that if there is no law against a particular behavior then it must be acceptable.

Abandoning our standards and accepting every kind of behavior leads to the inevitable lowering of standards. If we fail to define our moral boundaries, how can we protect them?

Some highly-paid entertainers display such a low standard of behavior that we should ridicule and scorn them instead of idolizing them. The only reason they can command those exorbitant salaries is because we watch their commercial endorsements and apparently buy whatever they tell us to. Either we are really dumb, or we are just numb after so much exposure to outrageous behavior.

The media play into the weirdos' hands, because evidently we like to watch that stuff. I suppose it makes us feel normal when we see such abnormal behavior. The problem arises when the two begin to merge and we can no longer tell them apart. We lose confidence in our ability to distinguish constructive from destructive behavior and we undermine our self respect.

More than ever before we have to compete on a global playing field, and we must have the best training. Our training includes education in technology, professionalism and self-confidence. We need to show the world that America means business, but it is hard to portray a business image with our pants falling down, our arms covered with tattoos and our hair painted blue.

RELINQUISHING COMMON SENSE

Many things are just common sense, and yet this idea seems all too unpopular. Whenever anything can be resolved through common sense, it should be. This saves time, money and agony. Don't expect the politicians, the lawyers or the media to like this approach, since their livelihoods depend on injecting complexity into every issue.

Our laws require that an accused person be acquitted if there is a reasonable doubt that <u>he</u> committed the crime. In our eagerness to be fair we have introduced so many other criteria, such as did the arresting officer read him his rights correctly, and was he able to understand English when his rights were read, etc. All these extra complications make us lose sight of the common sense approach—did <u>he</u> do it or could it have been someone else?

Our laws imply that an 18 year old is too irresponsible to drink, but is qualified to vote. This implies that it requires less maturity to vote than to drink. What a blatant double standard and lack of common sense on our part! We definitely do not want irresponsible people to vote.

It is unrealistic to pretend that all kids can learn at the same rate or even want to learn at the same rate. Separating kids by how quickly they learn, either by choice or aptitude, seems quite logical. Failure to teach every child at his maximum pace is not helping any of them, and certainly not helping America. Failure to recognize that people have different abilities is not compassionate; it is unrealistic and stupid. Our public school system has failed us and it is certainly not for lack of funding.

We want the best teachers money can buy, but unless we inject some common sense back into the program we will continue to trail behind many other countries, including some so-called developing countries that already have superior education systems. Foreign exchange students are often appalled at the low level of expectation in our schools. Far too much time is wasted and discipline seems almost non-existent. Incompetent teachers must be fired, and disruptive kids must be expelled. None of these things will happen unless parents take more responsibility for their kids' education.

EXCUSING STUPIDITY

We bend over backwards to make people feel good, even when they have every right to feel bad about themselves. We want people to feel good even when they behave stupidly. We not only excuse distorted behavior, but we excuse stupid behavior. It's like the emperor's new clothes—everyone can see it's stupid but no one wants to say it out loud for fear of being labeled intolerant. People do have a right to be stupid or make stupid decisions, but we should call it what it is so they understand there is a price to be paid.

Misusing a product is stupid, and does not automatically indicate the product is defective or unsafe. Generally the same product is used correctly by many other people. Stupid behavior generally arises from ignorance or carelessness, but if there is no penalty for this then what incentive is there for people to inform themselves or exercise more caution?

Taking drugs is stupid, getting pregnant unintentionally is stupid (rape victims excluded, of course), contracting HIV-Aids through promiscuous behavior is stupid. Stupidity comes in degrees, and when someone does something really stupid or irresponsible there should be a high price to pay. However, that does not mean we shouldn't feel compassion for some of them, and there are plenty of avenues for helping out. Again, this is our individual choice and has nothing to do with a collective responsibility.

ATTITUDE 9
HOOKED ON THE
MEDIA

It's too bad we cannot believe everything we hear, see and read. We want to trust people to tell us the truth and take them at face value. When we describe someone as "what you see is what you get" we generally mean it as a compliment. Unfortunately, this inherent trust that most of us have is regarded by some people as naiveté, and they take advantage of it. Crooks, con-artists and slick sales-people exploit this whenever they can. Without becoming too skeptical, we should recognize this as a vulnerable characteristic. Buying anything or believing anything comes with a certain risk factor.

The media also understand this characteristic very well, and use it to their full advantage. They can manipulate us like puppets. The media thrive on drama, and they love to make the news entertaining, instead of factual. Unfortunately, most people love sensation and find facts boring. Bad news sells far better than good news because it's generally more sensational.

The media depend on selling advertising spots, and advertisers depend on viewers, listeners and readers. The more viewers, the more expensive is the advertising. The caliber of the show or story is far less important than how popular it is. There will always be a certain number of viewers, no matter how worthless the program. We viewers hold all the cards, but we constantly squander our hand by encouraging the media to show mediocre programs.

The media are extremely self-serving. They sell confusion and division, just like the lawyers and politicians. The pundits have nothing to talk about if our lives are too simple and straightforward. The more differing opinions they can foster, the more drama there is. The more confusion they can inject into an argument, the more people will listen and watch in fascination.

MEDIA BIAS

It is expecting too much for the media to be unbiased and objective all the time. They have several methods of promoting their agenda. They can slant a story either way by just omitting certain information, so the casual reader or viewer gets a distorted perspective. They can play a story up or down, depending on their bias. They can saturate us with coverage of a story, even when most of us are not particularly interested in it. Conversely, they can give another story scant attention even when it should be a major issue, or they can suddenly drop a story when they wish to end the debate.

Similarly, they can promote the fortunes of almost anyone they choose—be it an entertainer or a politician—by giving him plenty of exposure, or they can give him the cold shoulder and he will remain anonymous. As the cliché says, there's no such thing as bad publicity. No matter what garbage or inaccuracies the media throw out, they know many of us will feed on it eagerly. It sometimes seems that we, the people, are the pawns in the game of chess that the media are playing.

POLITICAL CAMPAIGNS AND ELECTIONS

Political campaigns should be shorter and far less expensive. The media prolong and essentially control the whole process, and they make enormous profits from it. They should have no political agenda whatsoever, and should be completely objective. It is the media's job to relay the candidates' agendas to us, not to sway public opinion. They should not be choosing sides. We should not let them tell us what to think.

It should be prohibited for the media to conduct exit polls by asking people who they voted for and then publishing trends based on skin color, gender, age or any other label. These actions only perpetuate the divisions we have in our society. Why do the media make excuses for people who cannot fill out a ballot properly, even going so far as to call them disenfranchised? The truth is that if you cannot fill out a ballot you have no business voting.

Once the results are in, the media should respect the will of the people and not spin all kinds of hidden meanings and interpretations. The defeated candidates and their supporters should accept their loss with dignity, because any other reaction is Un-American. Unfortunately, losing with dignity seems to be quite uncommon.

ATTITUDE 10
COMPLACENCY

Complacency may be our worst habit and most dangerous attitude. We let a vociferous few dominate the debate on too many issues. Most people are just trying to make a living and take care of their lives, so they pay scant attention to these debates. The debates end up being defined and controlled by relatively few. We often don't like the decisions but shrug our shoulders because we missed the opportunity to get involved and influence the outcome.

We, the people, need to speak up when our common sense tells us that something isn't right. The talking heads can spew forth as many intellectual arguments as they want to, but we generally know what we think. If we just brush it off, our voices will not be heard, and then the assumption is that either we don't care what happens or we are happy with the end result.

We elect our representatives every so many years, and then all too often fail to stay abreast of their decisions. Although we elect them to make decisions on our behalf, that does not mean we give them a blank check. It requires constant monitoring and checking to ensure they are doing their job properly. We, the shareholders, actually hold all the power but, unless we exercise our power, it is useless. None of us can withdraw our investment in the company and, indeed, we are constantly reinvesting. We have a lot at stake and cannot afford to let the company squander our future.

Everyone should watch C-Span for a few hours a week to see how efficiently, or otherwise, the nation's business is being conducted. When we see our representatives indulge in posturing, grandstanding and bluffing, we should call their bluff. When we see them promoting special interest agendas, we should tell them to stop. When any special agenda does not appear to be in the best interests of the majority, we should also be suspicious that they have been paid off by the special interest group. Most importantly, we must have an efficient mechanism for registering our opinions so that the politicians know what we want. The more diverse our society becomes, the harder it is to agree on priorities, and priorities are normally what everything boils down to. We should give the politicians our priorities and allocate a budget for them. This should be part of the election process.

Just as we empower the government with a budget, most of us probably don't appreciate what a powerful tool we have with our own spending habits. We can make or break any policy or idea, any individual or group, any institution or company, simply by how and where we spend our money. As individuals, most of us could not have a significant impact, but collectively we certainly can. If we could only agree on the priorities!

We, the people, have tremendous power to change the course of events, but we are too passive. We should object loudly when we see juries awarding outrageous damages, when we see people flaunting outrageous behavior in public, and when we see illegal immigrants swarming across the border. We should ridicule union workers who strike for ever higher wages and exorbitant lifetime benefits, scorn sports players and entertainers who believe they can do no wrong, and ridicule people who too easily claim to have been offended. We should boycott companies that outsource all their jobs overseas, and boycott the media when we suspect they are not presenting the facts objectively.

VOTING

Voting is both a right and a privilege. Failure to vote does not relieve us of our ownership in the government. Millions of eligible voters are not even registered to vote. Millions of registered voters don't bother to vote—some because they are so disenchanted with the system that they have given up and don't think their voice counts for anything, others because they are so wrapped up in their own lives that they don't care who represents them. Both of these reasons are poor excuses, and we cannot hope to get control of the government when so many of us don't make the effort.

Even among those who do vote there are many who don't bother to research the candidates or the issues. The right to vote needs to be accompanied by the obligation to inform oneself about the issues and the candidates. Democracy can only function well if the voters are well informed. Uninformed voters are a liability, because they are most likely to support the candidates who promise them the most, particularly if they think they won't be the ones paying for these benefits.

Voting for our priorities and for a budget is perhaps more important than voting for our representatives. Once we had established the priorities and a budget, our representatives would have a clear mission and it would be easier for us all to stay on task. More people might be interested in voting if we had to vote on the priorities and the budget. These are complex questions, though, and perhaps the average American is unqualified to offer an opinion. It would be worthwhile trying to develop a system that encouraged this.

When we invest our hard earned money in the stock of a company, we do care how that company performs. How come we don't care how Uncle Sam Inc. performs, when most of us invest more in that company than anywhere else during our lifetimes? Whether or not we voted for the party in power, or whether we voted at all, we must still assume responsibility for our government. We cannot withdraw from the system, and neither should we want to. There are billions of people around the world who envy our right to vote, and many of them would die for that right. If we squander this right, we have no business calling ourselves Americans.

LET'S RECLAIM OUR HERITAGE

- Let's stop running from the attitudes our founding fathers valued so highly.

- Let's treat every American with equal dignity and respect, until they prove unworthy of such treatment. We are all Americans of equal standing in the eyes of God and the government.

- Let's quit arguing over our differences and focus on our common values. Diversity is only an asset if we don't exploit our differences.

- Let's expose hypocrisy wherever we see it, especially from the politicians and the media. When they speak with forked tongues, we must call them to task.

- Let's hold our politicians to the highest standard of ethics and integrity.

- Let's hold the government accountable for protecting majority rights and for not granting favors to anyone.

- Let's stop thinking the government is someone else. Let's teach our kids that Uncle Sam stands for "us".

- Let's understand that every dollar the government spends is ours, unless we leave it for our children to pay.

- Let's be proud owners of our government, but limit its power to control our lives.

- Let's take back our freedom and start assuming responsibility for our choices in life. Let's admit that we cannot have the former without the latter.

- Let's have the confidence to make our own decisions, without seeking a scapegoat when we fail.

- Let's prove to ourselves how generous and compassionate we really are by removing the government as the referee in the circle of charity.

- Let's quit suing every time we feel hurt or offended. Most of the time those paying the price are our fellow Americans—hopefully not the ones we had intended to punish.

- Let's admit that life comes with risks, and that the risks make our lives more challenging and worthwhile. Laws will not shield us from all risk.

- Let's value our corporations—large and small. They provide the jobs that our whole civilization depends on.

- Let's hold corporate executives to a very high standard of integrity, and severely punish anyone who abuses his authority, wealth or power.

- Let's encourage competition with other countries on a level playing field, but not be so quick to embrace all those imports. Our products probably cost more because our workers earn more, but those workers are our neighbors.

- Let's define our priorities, our values and our borders, and then defend them vigorously.

- Let's exercise better judgment in our choice of entertainment, and have higher expectations from our entertainers. Let's show the media that we want a balanced diet of news and entertainment, without their spin.

If we don't adjust our attitudes, I fear we will spiral into an ex-super power. We could even be heading towards a major philosophical divide and another civil war. Failure to reverse this tide is nothing short of Un-American.

978-0-595-38704-5
0-595-38704-7